16

3

0

0

Animal Lives

GIRAFFES

Sally Morgan

QED Publishing

First published in the UK in 2006 by
QED Publishing
A Quarto Group company
226 City Road
London EC1V 2TT

www.qed-publishing.co.uk

A Catalogue record for this book is
available from the British Library.

ISBN 1 84538 376 1

Written by Sally Morgan
Designed by Jonathan Vipond
Editor Hannah Ray
Picture Researcher Joanne Forrest Smith

Publisher Steve Evans
Art Director Zeta Davies
Editorial Director Jean Coppendale

Printed and bound in China

Picture Credits

Key: t=top, b=bottom, l=left, r=right,
FC = front cover

Alamy/Peter Arnold Inc 23 **Corbis**/Marcello
Calandrini 30tr, /John Conrad 16–17, /Nigel
J Dennis/Gallo Images 14–15, /Pat
Jerrold/Papilio 15tr, /Peter Johnson 6–7,
/Barbra Leigh 19tl, /Craig Lovell 30tl, /Joe
McDonald 1, /Jim Zuckerman 18; **Ecoscene**
/Dennis Johnson/Papilio 19, /Brian Cushing/
Papilio 11; **FLPA** /Frans Lanting/Minden
Pictures 28–29, /Yva Momatiuk & John
Eastcott/Minden Pictures 10; **Getty Images**
/Darrell Gulin FC, /jonathan & angela 24,
25, 27, /Nicholas Parfitt 22, /James Warwick
12–13; **NHPA** /Daryl Balfour 20–21, /Kevin
Schafer 4–5, 8, 26, /John Shaw 9, /James
Warwick 5tl, 16bl; **Still Pictures**/Michael
Fairchild 23, 30br.

Words in **bold** are
explained in the
Glossary on page 31.

Contents

The giraffe

The giraffe is the tallest animal in the world. It could look into a second-storey window without even having to stand on tiptoes! It has an incredibly long neck and four long legs. Its coat has a pattern of brown patches on a lighter, yellowish background.

Each giraffe has its own unique pattern of markings.

4

Cows and bulls

A male giraffe is called a bull and a female is called a cow. A young giraffe is called a calf.

A giraffe has a pair of horns and a number of bony lumps on its head.

Mammals

Giraffes belong to a group of animals called **mammals**. Mammals are animals that give birth to live young and produce milk to feed them. Other mammals include horses and elephants.

Giraffe

The bull grows as tall as 5.5m (to the top of its horns) and weighs up to 2000kg. The cow is slightly shorter at 4.5m and weighs about 1180kg.

fact

5

Where do you find giraffes?

Giraffes live only in Africa, south of the Sahara Desert. Large numbers are found in eastern and southern Africa. Giraffes were once common in the drier parts of Africa, too, such as the Sudan, Chad and Ethiopia. However, they were hunted for their meat. Sadly, the hunters killed too many giraffes and their numbers declined in these areas.

Giraffe

A giraffe's spots provide good **camouflage**. Many people have mistaken a giraffe for an old, dead tree.

fact

Giraffes live in small groups, called herds.

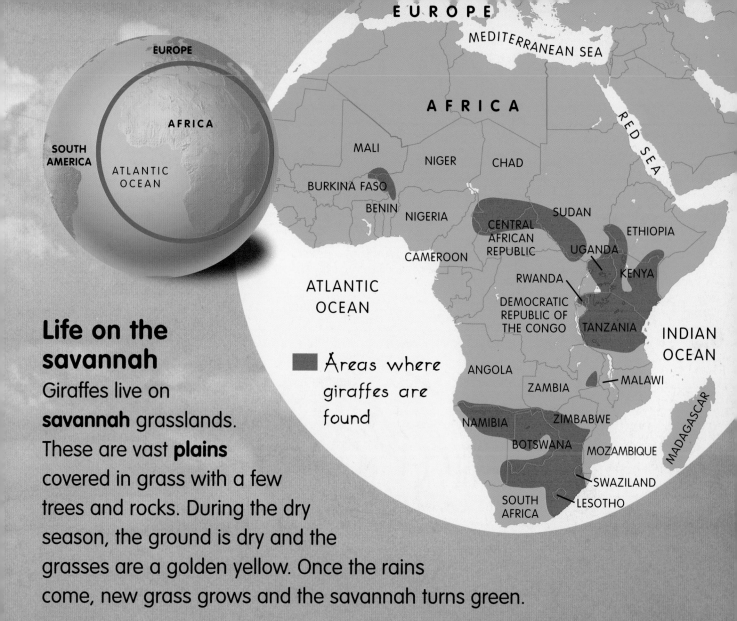

EUROPE

MEDITERRANEAN SEA

AFRICA

RED SEA

MALI

NIGER

CHAD

BURKINA FASO

BENIN

NIGERIA

CENTRAL
AFRICAN
REPUBLIC

SUDAN

ETHIOPIA

UGANDA

CAMEROON

RWANDA

KENYA

ATLANTIC
OCEAN

DEMOCRATIC
REPUBLIC OF
THE CONGO

TANZANIA

INDIAN
OCEAN

Areas where
giraffes are
found

ANGOLA

ZAMBIA

MALAWI

NAMIBIA

ZIMBABWE

MADAGASCAR

BOTSWANA

MOZAMBIQUE

SWAZILAND

SOUTH
AFRICA

LESOTHO

EUROPE

AFRICA

SOUTH
AMERICA

ATLANTIC
OCEAN

Life on the savannah

Giraffes live on **savannah** grasslands. These are vast **plains** covered in grass with a few trees and rocks. During the dry season, the ground is dry and the grasses are a golden yellow. Once the rains come, new grass grows and the savannah turns green.

Giraffe types

There is only one species, or type, of giraffe. However, there are some small differences between giraffes living in different parts of Africa. For this reason, the giraffe species is divided into nine **subspecies**. Many of these subspecies are named after the areas in which they live. For example, the Masai giraffe is from the Masai Mara, in Kenya.

The Masai giraffe has a pattern that looks like leaves.

Coat colours

As well as having different patterns, giraffes' coats may vary in colour, too. This is caused by the giraffes eating different plants and by where they live. Giraffes who live in drier, dustier places have paler yellow coats because they have **adapted** to their surroundings.

The Rothschild's giraffe is from Uganda and northern Kenya. It has deep brown, rectangular spots.

Giraffe

In the past, people thought the giraffe was a type of camel with leopard spots. Its Latin name, *Giraffa camelopardalis*, means camel-leopard.

fact

Beginning life

A female giraffe is ready to have her first calf when she is about five years old. After mating, she is **pregnant** for about 15 months. Giraffes give birth to one calf at a time. Twin calves are very rare.

A newborn calf weighs about 100kg and is just under 2m tall – that's as tall as an adult man! Calves grow quickly, as much as 2cm a day. Some double their height in just one year.

A newborn calf can stand up, walk and run within an hour of birth.

Protective mothers

Giraffes are very protective of their calves and will kick any animal that comes too close. Most giraffe calves are born at the same time of year. This is because more calves survive if they are born together, as **predators** cannot kill all of them.

As soon as it can stand, the newborn calf takes its first drink of milk.

Giraffe

Giraffes give birth in a place called a calving ground. Often a giraffe will return to where she was born to have her baby.

fact

11

Growing up

For the first few days of its life, the calf sits in the grass while its mother goes off to feed. When the calf is one or two weeks old, it is introduced to other giraffes.

The calf drinks its mothers' milk for 15 to 18 months, although it also eats leaves from about four months of age. The first few months are very dangerous for the young giraffes. They are preyed upon by predators such as hyenas, lions, leopards and hunting dogs.

Leaving mum

Young bull giraffes leave their mothers when they are about 15 months old. They join up with other bulls to form an all-male group. Young cow giraffes leave when they are about 18 months old, but they do not go very far and tend to stay in the same area as their mothers.

Older calves are left in a nursery group while their mothers go to feed. One cow stays behind to look after them.

13

Living in herds

Giraffes are sociable animals and live in a group called a herd. The herds are made up of individuals of one sex, for example the cows and their young, or a group of young bulls. There are usually between 12 and 15 animals in a herd. The only giraffes that prefer to live alone are the older bulls. These giraffes wander over the savannah, looking for cow giraffes.

Living in a herd helps to protect the giraffes against predators.

Moving between herds

The individuals in a herd do not stay together all the time. Giraffes wander off and join other herds in the area. However, some giraffes do stay together.

Giraffes that stay together may be mother and daughter, or unrelated giraffes that are friends.

Giraffe

The giraffe needs less sleep than almost any other mammal. It is thought to sleep for between 20 minutes and two hours in every 24 hours.

fact

Home range

Herds of cow giraffes live in a large area that is called a **home range**. However, unlike mammals such as lions, they do not guard the boundaries of their home range. The cows tend to stay in the central part of their home range when looking for food. They get to know this area very well and so they are more relaxed. When they move into the outer parts of their home range, they are more alert because they do not know it so well.

Giraffes find all their food and water in their home range.

Wanderers

Bull giraffes either live on their own or with other bulls, depending on how old they are. They move through the home ranges of the cows. The young bulls are great wanderers and they will travel long distances in only a few months.

Bull giraffes that live on their own may travel tens of kilometres every day.

17

Feeding on leaves

Giraffes are plant eaters, or **herbivores**. They are **browsing** animals that feed on the leaves of trees. Often, trees have long thorns to stop browsing animals from eating their leaves. However, thorns do not stop giraffes! The giraffes pull the leaves and thorns into their mouths. Then they produce lots of saliva to help chew and swallow the thorny mixture. As well as leaves and thorns, they eat flowers, fruits and seeds, too.

You can tell a bull from a cow by the way it eats. Cows tend to bend their necks, while bulls eat at full stretch.

Giraffes use their tongues and thick lips to pull leaves into their mouths.

Giraffe

The tongue of the giraffe is very long. It is about 46cm – that's as long as a child's arm!

fact

19

Bending over

Believe it or not, the long neck of the giraffe has the same number of bones as a person's neck – that's just seven **vertebrae**. However, each vertebra of the giraffe is much longer than the vertebrae of a human.

Big hearts

The heart of a giraffe is very large so it can pump blood all the way up to its head. There are special **valves** in the blood vessels of the neck that stop blood rushing to the giraffe's head when it bends over.

Drinking danger

Giraffes get most of their water from the leaves they eat but sometimes they have to drink from a river or water hole. To reach down, they move their front feet apart, bend their knees and lower their necks. This is a very dangerous time for giraffes. It is easy for a predator, such as a crocodile, to grab hold of a giraffe when it is bent over.

Giraffes take turns to watch for predators.

Giraffe fact

The heart of a giraffe weighs 10kg, that's about 25 times heavier than a human heart.

21

Giraffe senses

Senses are very important to all mammals and this is also true of giraffes. The giraffe uses its senses to find food, watch for predators and keep an eye on its young.

The giraffe has no problem seeing over the long grasses of the savannah.

Seeing

Giraffes have excellent eyesight. One of the advantages of being so tall is that they can see over long distances, too. Their eyes are positioned to the side of their heads, which means they can see predators creeping up behind them.

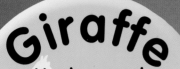

Giraffe

Herds several kilometres apart on the savannah can often see each other and keep in contact.

fact

Hearing and smelling

Giraffes' hearing and sense of smell are also good. They can move their ears to follow the direction of a sound. The bulls have a particularly good sense of smell and this allows them to find cows that are ready to mate.

Giraffes do not have very good night vision, so they are active only on moonlit nights.

Giraffe movement

Giraffes are **hoofed** mammals but they walk in a different way from other mammals, such as horses or antelope. Most four-legged mammals walk forwards by moving one leg on each side at a time. Giraffes, however, swing both legs on one side of their body forward at the same time and then they move the legs on the other side.

The way in which a giraffe walks is called pacing.

Galloping

When giraffes gallop, both back legs are moved forwards together, then the front legs are moved forwards. The heavy head of the giraffe moves forward with each powerful stride, then swings back. This helps the giraffe to balance so that it does not fall over.

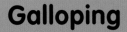

Giraffe

Giraffes can gallop at speeds of up to 60km/h. Calves can gallop even faster.

fact

Galloping giraffes can move quickly over the savannah.

25

Communication

Giraffes are mostly silent animals but they can make a variety of sounds. These sounds include grunts, snorts, moans and hisses. A cow looking for her calf will bellow loudly. Sight also plays a role in giraffe communication. This is because they recognize each other from the pattern of their markings.

Giraffe
Scientists believe that other animals stay near giraffes because they can see danger from a distance.
fact

Calves bleat and make mewing sounds, a bit like a cat.

Necking

Young bulls work out their position within a herd by necking. This is when they wrap their necks around each other and push and pull.

Fighting

Very rarely, there is a fight. Two fighting bulls smash their heads against each other's bodies. Fortunately, the skull of the bull is extra thick, so it is not damaged.

Necking is the giraffe version of arm wrestling.

27

Giraffes under threat

Over the last 100 years, the number of giraffes has fallen. Hunting has reduced the number of giraffes living in the northern parts of Africa. There are also very few giraffes left in West Africa. However, in the rest of Africa, giraffes are doing well and their numbers are on the increase.

Giraffes are also suffering from a loss of their **habitat**. Areas of the savannah are being used to graze sheep and goats. It is also being ploughed up for farmland and built on to create new towns and cities.

Giraffe
Studies show that there are only about 450 Rothschild's giraffes left in the wild.

fact

These tourists have travelled to Africa to watch wildlife, such as giraffes.

28

Conservation

One way to conserve the giraffes is to protect their habitat from disturbance and damage. Areas of savannah can be made into National Parks and game reserves. Tourists come to see giraffes in their natural habitat and they bring in valuable money for the local people.

Life cycle

A cow giraffe is pregnant for 15 months and gives birth to a single calf. The calf stays with its mother for about 15–18 months. A cow is ready to breed when she is 5 years old. Bulls are ready to mate when they reach 4 years old. A cow has 6 or 7 calves in her lifetime. Giraffes live up to 25 years in the wild and 28 years in captivity.

Adult

Glossary

adapted an animal that has changed to suit the environment in which it lives

browsing when an animal feeds on leaves from trees and shrubs, rather than on grass on the ground

camouflage when an animal blends in with its surroundings

habitat the place in which an animal lives

herbivore an animal that eats plants

home range an area where a giraffe spends its life

hoof the hard covering over the end of the toes of mammals, such as horses, giraffes and deer

mammal an animal that gives birth to live young, rather than laying eggs. Female mammals produce milk to feed their young

plain a large area of flat land

predator an animal that hunts other animals

pregnant a female animal that has a baby or babies developing inside her

savannah a grassy plain found in tropical parts of the world

subspecies groups within a species that look slightly different from each other

valve a flap within a blood vessel that stops the blood from flowing backwards

vertebrae (singular vertebra) the small bones that make up the back bone, including the neck

31

Index